Homestyle Casseroles

Table of Contents

Tuna Penne Casserole

   6 ounces uncooked penne pasta
   1 can (10¾ ounces) condensed cream of chicken soup, undiluted
   1 can (6 ounces) tuna, drained and flaked
   1 cup (4 ounces) shredded sharp Cheddar cheese
   ½ cup celery slices
   ½ cup milk
   ¼ cup mayonnaise
   1 can (4 ounces) sliced water chestnuts, drained
   1 jar (2 ounces) chopped pimientos, drained
   ½ teaspoon salt
      Dash black pepper
      Pinch celery seeds

1. Preheat oven to 350°F. Spray 2-quart casserole with nonstick cooking spray.

2. Cook pasta according to package directions; drain. Return to saucepan. Add soup, tuna, cheese, celery, milk, mayonnaise, water chestnuts, pimientos, salt, pepper and celery seeds; mix well. Transfer to prepared casserole.

3. Bake 25 minutes or until hot and bubbly.   *Makes 6 servings*

Sausage, Beef & Bean Casserole

- **1 pound sweet or hot Italian pork sausage, cut into 1-inch pieces**
- **½ pound ground beef**
- **1 small onion, chopped (about ¼ cup)**
- **1 bag (6 ounces) fresh baby spinach leaves**
- **1 can (10¾ ounces) CAMPBELL'S® Condensed Cream of Mushroom Soup (Regular or 98% Fat Free)**
- **¼ cup milk**
- **1 can (about 15 ounces) white kidney beans (cannellini), rinsed and drained**
- **1 cup PEPPERIDGE FARM® Herb Seasoned Stuffing**
- **½ cup crumbled blue cheese or shredded Cheddar cheese**

1. Heat the oven to 350°F.

2. Cook the sausage, beef and onion in a 12-inch oven-safe skillet until the sausage and beef are well browned, stirring often to break up beef. Pour off any fat. Stir in the spinach and cook until the spinach is wilted.

3. Stir the soup, milk and beans in the skillet.

4. Stir the stuffing and cheese in a small bowl. Sprinkle around the inside edge of the skillet.

5. Bake for 30 minutes or until the sausage mixture is hot and bubbling.

Makes 6 servings

Kitchen Tip: If your skillet has a handle that is not oven-safe, cover it with aluminum foil to protect it in the oven.

Prep Time: 15 minutes
Cook Time: 30 minutes
Total Time: 45 minutes

Glazed Pork Chops with Corn Stuffing

1³/₄ **cups SWANSON® Chicken Stock**
 ¹/₈ **teaspoon ground red pepper**
 1 cup frozen whole kernel corn
 1 stalk celery, chopped (about ¹/₂ cup)
 1 medium onion, chopped (about ¹/₂ cup)
 4 cups PEPPERIDGE FARM® Corn Bread Stuffing
    Vegetable cooking spray
 6 boneless pork chops, ³/₄-inch thick (about 1¹/₂ pounds)
 2 tablespoons packed brown sugar
 2 teaspoons spicy-brown mustard

1. Heat the stock, red pepper, corn, celery and onion in a 3-quart saucepan over medium heat to a boil. Remove the saucepan from the heat. Add the stuffing and mix lightly.

2. Spray a 3-quart shallow baking dish with the cooking spray. Spoon the stuffing into the baking dish. Top with the pork. Stir the brown sugar and mustard in a small bowl until the mixture is smooth. Spread the brown sugar mixture over the pork.

3. Bake at 400°F. for 30 minutes or until the pork is cooked through.

Makes 6 servings

Prep Time: 15 minutes
Bake Time: 30 minutes
Total Time: 45 minutes

Hearty Lasagna Rolls

1½ pounds ground beef
1 cup chopped fresh mushrooms
1 medium onion, finely chopped
1 small carrot, finely chopped
1 clove garlic, finely chopped
¼ cup dry red wine or beef broth
⅛ teaspoon cayenne pepper (optional)
2 cups shredded mozzarella cheese
1 egg, lightly beaten
5 tablespoons grated Parmesan cheese, divided
1 jar (1 pound 8 ounces) RAGÚ® Robusto!® Pasta Sauce
12 ounces lasagna noodles, cooked and drained

1. Preheat oven to 350°F. In 12-inch skillet, brown ground beef over medium-high heat; drain. Stir in mushrooms, onion, carrot and garlic; cook over medium heat, stirring occasionally, until vegetables are tender. Stir in wine and cayenne pepper; cook over high heat 3 minutes. Remove from heat; let stand 10 minutes.

2. In medium bowl, thoroughly combine ground beef mixture, mozzarella cheese, egg and 2 tablespoons Parmesan cheese. In 13×9-inch baking dish, evenly pour 2 cups Pasta Sauce. Evenly spread ⅓ cup ground beef filling over each lasagna noodle. Carefully roll up noodles. Place seam-side-down in baking dish. Evenly spread remaining sauce over lasagna rolls. Bake, covered, 40 minutes. Sprinkle with remaining 3 tablespoons Parmesan cheese and bake, uncovered, 5 minutes or until bubbling.   *Makes 6 servings*

Biscuit-Topped Chicken Pot Pie

1½ pounds boneless skinless chicken breasts, cut into 1-inch chunks
¼ cup chicken broth
1 bag (16 ounces) frozen mixed vegetables, such as cauliflower, carrots, broccoli, zucchini and red bell pepper
1 can (10¾ ounces) condensed cream of chicken soup, undiluted
4 tablespoons grated Parmesan cheese, divided
1 teaspoon dried thyme
½ teaspoon black pepper
1½ cups biscuit baking mix
½ cup milk

1. Preheat oven to 400°F. Combine chicken and broth in large saucepan; bring to a boil over high heat. Reduce heat; simmer 8 minutes or until chicken is cooked through, stirring occasionally. Stir in vegetables, soup, 2 tablespoons cheese, thyme and pepper; mix well. Cook until heated through. Transfer mixture to 8-inch square baking dish.

2. Combine baking mix and milk in small bowl; mix just until dry ingredients are moistened. Drop batter by heaping tablespoonfuls over hot chicken mixture; top with remaining 2 tablespoons cheese.

3. Bake 14 to 16 minutes or until bubbly and biscuits are golden brown.

Makes 6 servings

Tip: Freeze leftovers for another day. To reheat a frozen casserole, unwrap it and microwave, covered, on HIGH for 20 to 30 minutes, stirring once or twice during cooking. Allow to stand 5 minutes before serving.

13

Turkey Veggie Tetrazzini

8 ounces dry whole wheat spaghetti

1 package (16 ounces) frozen Italian-style vegetable blend (broccoli, red peppers, mushrooms and onions)

1 tablespoon olive oil

¼ cup all-purpose flour

½ teaspoon garlic powder

¼ teaspoon salt

¼ teaspoon ground black pepper

1 can (14.5 fluid ounces) reduced sodium chicken broth

1 can (12 fluid ounces) NESTLÉ® CARNATION® Evaporated Lowfat 2% Milk

¾ cup (2.25 ounces) shredded Parmesan cheese, divided

2 cups cooked, chopped turkey breast meat

PREHEAT oven to 350°F. Lightly grease 13×9-inch baking dish.

PREPARE pasta according to package directions, adding frozen vegetables to boiling pasta water for last minute of cooking time; drain. Return pasta and vegetables to cooking pot.

MEANWHILE, HEAT oil in medium saucepan over medium heat. Stir in flour, garlic powder, salt and pepper; cook, stirring constantly, for 1 minute. Remove from heat; gradually stir in broth. Return to heat; bring to boil over medium heat, stirring constantly. Stir in evaporated milk and *½ cup* cheese; cook over low heat until cheese melts. Remove from heat. Stir in turkey.

POUR cheese sauce over pasta and vegetables; mix lightly. Pour into prepared baking dish. Sprinkle with *remaining ¼ cup* cheese.

BAKE for 20 to 25 minutes or until lightly browned. Serve immediately.

Makes 12 servings

Prep Time: 20 minutes
Cooking Time: 45 minutes

Gumbo Casserole

2 cans (10¾ ounces each) CAMPBELL'S® Condensed Light Soups
Chicken Gumbo Soup
1 soup can water
1 teaspoon dried minced onion
½ teaspoon Cajun seasoning
½ teaspoon garlic powder
1 cup frozen okra, thawed
¾ cup uncooked instant white rice
½ pound cooked ham, diced (about 1½ cups)
½ pound cooked shrimp, peeled and deveined

1. Heat the oven to 375°F. Stir the soup, water, onion, Cajun seasoning, garlic powder, okra, rice, ham and shrimp in a 2-quart casserole.

2. Bake for 35 minutes or until the gumbo is hot and bubbling. Stir the gumbo before serving. *Makes 4 servings*

Kitchen Tip: Try stirring in a little diced andouille sausage for even more Cajun-style flavor!

Prep Time: 15 minutes
Cook Time: 35 minutes
Total Time: 50 minutes

Pastitsio

1½ **pounds ground beef**
1 **can (about 14 ounces) diced tomatoes with garlic and onion**
1 **can (8 ounces) tomato sauce**
2 **tablespoons Greek seasoning, divided**
1 **pound uncooked penne pasta or elbow macaroni**
¼ **cup (½ stick) butter**
¼ **cup all-purpose flour**
2 **cups milk**
2 **eggs, lightly beaten**
½ **cup grated Parmesan cheese**

1. Brown ground beef in large nonstick skillet over medium heat, stirring to break up meat. Drain fat. Add tomatoes, tomato sauce and 1½ tablespoons Greek seasoning. Reduce heat; simmer, uncovered, 25 to 30 minutes.

2. Meanwhile, cook pasta according to package directions. Drain; transfer to 2-quart casserole. Preheat oven to 350°F.

3. Melt butter in medium saucepan over medium heat. Stir in flour; cook 2 minutes. Whisk in milk and remaining ½ tablespoon Greek seasoning; cook just until sauce thickens. Remove from heat. Stir about ¼ cup sauce into eggs. Add egg mixture back to sauce in pan. Cook over medium heat until mixture thickens. *Do not boil.* Stir in cheese.

4. Stir ½ cup cheese sauce into pasta. Top with meat sauce and remaining cheese sauce.

5. Bake 30 to 40 minutes or until top is golden. Let stand 15 minutes before serving. *Makes 6 servings*

Chicken Enchilada Casserole

  1 teaspoon olive oil
  1 cup chopped red onion
  1 can (4 ounces) diced mild green chiles
  2 cans (10 ounces each) mild enchilada sauce
12 ounces shredded cooked chicken
  $\frac{2}{3}$ cup sliced green onions
12 (6-inch) corn tortillas
  $\frac{3}{4}$ cup (3 ounces) shredded Mexican cheese blend
  $\frac{1}{2}$ cup sour cream (optional)

1. Preheat oven to 350°F. Heat oil in large nonstick skillet over medium-high heat. Add red onion and chiles; cook and stir 4 to 5 minutes or until red onion is tender. Stir in sauce, chicken and green onions.

2. Spray 2½-quart oval casserole with nonstick cooking spray. Place 4 tortillas in bottom of casserole. Spoon 2 cups chicken mixture over tortillas; top with ¼ cup cheese. Top with 4 tortillas, 1 cup chicken mixture and ¼ cup cheese. Repeat with remaining 4 tortillas, chicken mixture and cheese.

3. Cover and bake 20 minutes. Uncover and bake 10 minutes or until thoroughly heated. Let stand 10 minutes before serving. Serve with sour cream, if desired. *Makes 8 servings*

Easy Shepherd's Pie

1½ **pounds lean ground beef**
  1 **cup chopped onion**
  2 **cups frozen green beans, thawed**
  1 **can (14.5 ounces) diced tomatoes, drained**
  1 **jar (12 ounces) beef gravy**
  1 **cup frozen corn niblets, thawed**
  1 **teaspoon dried thyme leaves**
  ½ **teaspoon salt**
  1 **package SIMPLY POTATOES® Mashed Potatoes**

1. Heat oven to 375°F. Spray 2½- to 3-quart casserole baking dish with nonstick cooking spray.

2. In 12-inch skillet cook ground beef and onion until browned; drain grease. Add beans, tomatoes, gravy, corn, thyme and salt. Cook until heated through. Spoon beef mixture into casserole dish. Spread **Simply Potatoes®** evenly over beef mixture. Bake 30 to 35 minutes or until edges are bubbly. Remove from oven.

3. Heat broiler. Broil casserole 4 to 6 inches from heat, 3 to 5 minutes, until **Simply Potatoes®** are lightly browned.   *Makes 6 servings*

Prep Time: 15 minutes
Total Time: 55 minutes

Baked Ziti with Pumpkin & Sausage

Nonstick cooking spray
4 cups (12 ounces) dry regular or whole-wheat ziti
1 can (15 ounces) LIBBY'S® 100% Pure Pumpkin
2 tablespoons all-purpose flour
1 teaspoon garlic powder
½ teaspoon salt
¼ teaspoon ground nutmeg
⅛ teaspoon cayenne pepper
1 can (12 fluid ounces) NESTLÉ® CARNATION® Evaporated Fat Free Milk
4 links (12 ounces) fully-cooked Italian-seasoned chicken sausage, cut into ¼-inch slices
1 package (6 ounces) or about 4 cups pre-washed baby spinach
1 cup (4 ounces) shredded part-skim or 2% milk reduced-fat mozzarella cheese
1 cup (1½ ounces) shredded Parmesan cheese

PREHEAT oven to 425°F. Spray 4-quart baking dish with nonstick cooking spray.

PREPARE pasta according to package directions. *Reserve ½ cup pasta cooking water and set aside for later use.* Drain pasta; return to pot.

MEANWHILE, COMBINE pumpkin, flour, garlic powder, salt, nutmeg and cayenne pepper in medium skillet over medium heat. Slowly add evaporated milk, stirring until smooth. Cook, stirring occasionally, for 2 to 3 minutes or until mixture begins to thicken slightly. Pour over pasta in pot. Add sausage and *reserved* pasta cooking water; stir well.

SPREAD *half* of the pasta mixture into prepared baking dish. Top with spinach. Cover with *remaining* pasta mixture. Lightly spray piece of foil with nonstick cooking spray. Cover ziti with foil, greased-side-down.

BAKE for 20 minutes or until heated through. Combine mozzarella and Parmesan cheeses in small bowl. Remove foil; sprinkle with cheese mixture. Bake, uncovered, for an additional 5 minutes or until cheese is melted. *Makes 12 servings*

Prep Time: 20 minutes
Baking Time: 25 minutes

Easy Layered Tomato Pesto Casserole

    Vegetable cooking spray
  2 cans (10¾ ounces each) CAMPBELL'S® Condensed Tomato Soup
1½ cups milk
  3 eggs
  1 container (7 ounces) prepared pesto sauce
  8 slices PEPPERIDGE FARM® Farmhouse™ Hearty White Bread
  1 package (8 ounces) shredded Italian cheese blend

1. Spray a 3-quart shallow baking dish with cooking spray. Stir the soup, milk and eggs in a medium bowl with a fork. Spoon ½ **cup** of the soup mixture into the prepared dish.

2. Spread **about 1 tablespoon** pesto sauce on **each** bread slice. Place **4** slices in the dish. Top with ½ **cup** of the cheese. Pour about **half** of the soup mixture over the bread and cheese. Repeat layers with the remaining bread slices, ½ **cup** cheese and the remaining soup mixture, making sure the bread is coated with the soup mixture.

3. Bake at 350°F. for 40 minutes or until center is set. Sprinkle with the remaining cheese. Let stand for 5 minutes or until the cheese is melted.

Makes 8 servings

Prep Time: 10 minutes
Cook Time: 45 minutes
Total Time: 55 minutes

Wild Rice & Chicken Casserole

1 package (6 ounces) long grain & wild rice mix
2 tablespoons butter
½ cup chopped onion
½ cup chopped celery
2 cups cubed cooked chicken
1 can (10¾ ounces) condensed cream of mushroom soup, undiluted
½ cup sour cream
⅓ cup dry white wine
½ teaspoon curry powder

1. Preheat oven to 350°F.

2. Prepare rice mix according to package directions.

3. Meanwhile, melt butter in large skillet over medium heat. Add onion and celery; cook and stir until tender. Stir in rice, chicken, soup, sour cream, wine and curry powder. Transfer mixture to 2-quart casserole.

4. Bake 40 minutes or until heated through.   *Makes 4 to 6 servings*

Salmon Veg•All® Pasta Bake

3 cups cooked small shell pasta

1 can (14¾ ounces) pink salmon, drained or 1 pound cooked salmon

1 can (15 ounces) VEG•ALL® Original Mixed Vegetables, drained

1 can (10¾ ounces) condensed cream of mushroom soup

¼ teaspoon pepper

½ cup dry bread crumbs

Preheat oven to 350°F.

In large bowl, combine pasta, salmon, Veg•All, soup and pepper.

Pour into greased 3-quart casserole.

Bake 25 minutes or until hot. Sprinkle bread crumbs over top; bake, uncovered, 10 minutes more.   *Makes 6 servings*

Acknowledgments

The publisher would like to thank the companies and organizations listed below for the use of their recipes and photographs in this publication.

Campbell Soup Company

Crystal Farms®

Nestlé USA

Unilever

Veg•All®